The National Committee of Inquiry into **Higher Education**

Summary Report

Exeter

University of Plym OF

Subject to status this
via your Voy

http://voyage

Exeter tel
Exmouth te
Plymouth te

Contents

Chairman's foreword

1   We were appointed with bipartisan support by the Secretaries of State for Education and Employment, Wales, Scotland, and Northern Ireland on 10 May 1996 to make recommendations on how the purposes, shape, structure, size and funding of higher education, including support for students, should develop to meet the needs of the United Kingdom over the next 20 years, recognising that higher education embraces teaching, learning, scholarship and research. We were asked to report by the summer of 1997. Our full terms of reference are set out on pages 5 and 6.

2   We now submit our report. In doing so, we thank those who were members of the working groups we created to study and advise on particular issues, and in particular the members of our Scottish Committee, whose advice to us is published as part of our report. We are indebted to all those who gave evidence, both oral and written. We are grateful to those in higher education in this country and in the countries we visited for being so open with us as we sought to inform ourselves and develop policies for the future. Most of all we are indebted to our secretariat and in particular to our secretary, Shirley Trundle, who served us with distinction and far beyond the call of duty. We were indeed fortunate in having such a team.

3   I am personally much indebted to all my colleagues on the Committee, of whom I asked far more than they can have envisaged when they agreed to join it. This report is very much the work of all of us.

An introductory comment

4   We were appointed to advise on the long term development of higher education. But we express here our concern that the long term wellbeing of higher education should not be damaged by the needs of the short term.

5   We are particularly concerned about planned further reductions in the unit of funding for higher education. If these are carried forward, it will have been halved in 25 years. We believe that this would damage both the quality and effectiveness of higher education. We are also concerned about some other immediate needs, especially in relation to research.

6   We recognise the need for new sources of finance for higher education to respond to these problems and to provide for growth. We therefore recommend that students enter into an obligation to make contributions to the cost of their higher education once they are in work. Inescapably these contributions lie in the future. But there are pressing needs which we identify in the Report in the years 1998/99 and 1999/2000. We urge the Government to respond to these in its decisions on funding, by giving credit for the value embedded in the commitments given by students to provide for their education. The present public expenditure and accounting practice does not provide for this: it therefore fails to recognise value that is properly recognised in normal commercial accounts, and leads to costly arrangements for securing that value by sale of the loan book, which can be ill afforded.

7   Much of our report is concerned with material things and with the central role of higher education in the economy. It would be surprising were it not so. But throughout we have kept in mind the values that characterise higher education and which are fundamental to any understanding of it. They were well expressed by John Masefield in an address at the University of Sheffield in 1946. Speaking of a university, he said, as we would now say of higher education as a whole:

> 'It is a place where those who hate ignorance may strive to know, where those who perceive truth may strive to make others see; where seekers and learners alike, banded together in the search for knowledge, will honour thought in all its finer ways, will welcome thinkers in distress or in exile, will uphold ever the dignity of thought and learning and will exact standards in these things.'

8   It must continue to be so.

Ron Dearing

The National Committee of Inquiry into Higher Education

Terms of reference

To make recommendations on how the purposes, shape, structure, size and funding of higher education, including support for students, should develop to meet the needs of the United Kingdom over the next 20 years, recognising that higher education embraces teaching, learning, scholarship and research.

The Committee should report by the summer of 1997.
The Committee should take account of the context in Annex A

The Committee should have regard, within the constraints of the Government's other spending priorities and affordability, to the following principles:
- there should be maximum participation in initial higher education by young and mature students and in lifetime learning by adults, having regard to the needs of individuals, the nation and the future labour market;
- students should be able to choose between a diverse range of courses, institutions, modes and locations of study;
- standards of degrees and other higher education qualifications should be at least maintained, and assured;
- the effectiveness of teaching and learning should be enhanced;
- learning should be increasingly responsive to employment needs and include the development of general skills, widely valued in employment;
- higher education's contribution to basic, strategic and applied research should be maintained and enhanced, particularly in subjects where UK research has attained international standards of excellence or in Technology Foresight priority areas;
- arrangements for student support should be fair and transparent, and support the principles above;
- higher education should be able to recruit, retain and motivate staff of the appropriate calibre;
- value for money and cost-effectiveness should be obtained in the use of resources.

Annex A to the terms of reference

The Committee should take account of the following context:
- demand for higher education from suitably qualified applicants of all ages is growing as more people achieve qualifications at level 3 and more of those who already have higher level qualifications look to upgrade or update them;
- there is a growing diversity of students in higher education with a growing number of mature entrants, part-timers, and women students;
- higher education continues to have a key role in developing the powers of the mind, and in advancing understanding and learning through scholarship and research;

- the UK must now compete in increasingly competitive international markets where the proliferation of knowledge, technological advances and the information revolution mean that labour market demand for those with higher level education and training is growing, particularly in business, and that there is a greater premium on the products of the country's research base;
- many of our international competitors are aiming to improve the contribution their higher education systems make to their economic performance;
- higher education has a key role in delivering national policies and meeting industry's needs for science, engineering and technology in research and postgraduate training;
- a flourishing higher education system is important for all sectors of the economy and essential to the NHS and the education service, supplying qualified manpower, research and innovation, and continuing professional development;
- through scholarship and research, higher education provides a national resource of knowledge and expertise for the benefit of out international competitiveness and quality of life, and provides a basis for responding to social and economic change through innovation and lifelong learning;
- higher education continues to have a role in the nation's social, moral and spiritual life; in transmitting citizenship and culture in all its variety; and in enabling personal development for the benefit of individuals and society as a whole;
- higher education is a major contributor to local, regional and national economic growth and regeneration;
- there are distinctive features of higher education in different parts of the UK;
- links between higher education and other parts of the education and training system, particularly further education, are increasing in importance;
- links between higher education in the UK and elsewhere in the world are growing, as the international mobility of students and staff increases;
- higher education is an important educational export in its own right;
- new technology is opening up the possibility of new forms of teaching and learning, and higher education is increasingly delivered in the work-place and in the home through distance-learning;
- the Government has legislated to enable private financial institutions to offer loans to students on similar terms to those offered by the Student Loans Company;
- there have already been reviews of a number of areas likely to be of interest to the Committee, for example of the national framework of qualifications and of credit accumulation and transfer, of postgraduate education, and of the dual support arrangements for research funding.

Members of the National Committee

Professor John Arbuthnott	Principal and Vice-Chancellor of the University of Strathclyde
Baroness Dean of Thornton-le-Fylde	(formerly Brenda Dean)
Sir Ron Dearing	(Chairman)
Ms Judith Evans	Departmental Director of Personnel Policy, Sainsbury's
Sir Ron Garrick	Managing Director and Chief Executive of Weir Group
Sir Geoffrey Holland	Vice-Chancellor of the University of Exeter
Professor Diana Laurillard	Pro Vice-Chancellor (Technology Development) of the Open University
Mrs Pamela Morris	Headteacher, The Blue School, Wells
Sir Ronald Oxburgh	Rector of Imperial College of Science, Technology and Medicine
Dr David Potter	Chairman of Psion plc
Sir George Quigley	Chairman of Ulster Bank
Sir William Stubbs	Rector of the London Institute
Sir Richard Sykes	Chairman and Chief Executive of Glaxo Wellcome plc
Professor David Watson	Director of the University of Brighton
Professor Sir David Weatherall	Regius Professor of Medicine at the University of Oxford
Professor Adrian Webb	Vice-Chancellor of the University of Glamorgan
Mr Simon Wright	Academic Affairs Officer, Students Union, the University of Wales College of Cardiff

Secretary to the National Committee

Mrs Shirley Trundle	Department for Education and Employment

Introduction

1. This summary of our main report includes some of our key recommendations. You are strongly recommended to read as well the full list of our recommendations at the back of the summary.

A vision for 20 years: the learning society

2. Our title, 'Higher Education in the learning society', reflects the vision that informs this report. Over the next 20 years, the United Kingdom must create a society committed to learning throughout life. That commitment will be required from individuals, the state, employers and providers of education and training. Education is life enriching and desirable in its own right. It is fundamental to the achievement of an improved quality of life in the UK.

3. It should, therefore, be a national policy objective to be world class both in learning at all levels and in a range of research of different kinds. In higher education, this aspiration should be realised through a new compact involving institutions and their staff, students, government, employers and society in general. We see the historic boundaries between vocational and academic education breaking down, with increasingly active partnerships between higher education institutions and the worlds of industry, commerce and public service. In such a compact, each party should recognise its obligation to the others.

4. Over the next 20 years, we see higher education gaining in strength through the pursuit of quality and a commitment to high standards. Higher education will make a distinctive contribution to the development of a learning society through teaching, scholarship and research. National need and demand for higher education will drive a resumed expansion of student numbers – young and mature, full-time and part-time. But over the next two decades, higher education will face challenges as well as opportunities. The effectiveness of its response will determine its future.

5. That future will require higher education in the UK to:
    - encourage and enable all students – whether they demonstrate the highest intellectual potential or whether they have struggled to reach the threshold of higher education – to achieve beyond their expectations;
    - safeguard the rigour of its awards, ensuring that UK qualifications meet the needs of UK students and have standing throughout the world;
    - be at the leading edge of world practice in effective learning and teaching;
    - undertake research that matches the best in the world, and make its benefits available to the nation;
    - ensure that its support for regional and local communities is at least comparable to that provided by higher education in competitor nations;
    - sustain a culture which demands disciplined thinking, encourages curiosity, challenges existing ideas and generates new ones;
    - be part of the conscience of a democratic society, founded on respect for the rights of the individual and the responsibilities of the individual to society as a whole;

- be explicit and clear in how it goes about its business, be accountable to students and to society, and seek continuously to improve its own performance.

6. To achieve this, higher education will depend on:
   - professional, committed members of staff who are appropriately trained, respected and rewarded;
   - a diverse range of autonomous, well-managed institutions with a commitment to excellence in the achievement of their distinctive missions.

7. The higher education sector will comprise a community of free-standing institutions dedicated to the creation of a learning society and the pursuit of excellence in their diverse missions. It will include institutions of world renown and it must be a conscious objective of national policy that the UK should continue to have such institutions. Other institutions will see their role as supporting regional or local needs. Some will see themselves as essentially research oriented; others will be predominantly engaged in teaching. But all will be committed to scholarship and to excellence in the management of learning and teaching.

8. Higher education is fundamental to the social, economic and cultural health of the nation. It will contribute not only through the intellectual development of students and by equipping them for work, but also by adding to the world's store of knowledge and understanding, fostering culture for its own sake, and promoting the values that characterise higher education: respect for evidence; respect for individuals and their views; and the search for truth. Equally, part of its task will be to accept a duty of care for the wellbeing of our democratic civilisation, based on respect for the individual and respect by the individual for the conventions and laws which provide the basis of a civilised society.

9. There is growing interdependence between students, institutions, the economy, employers and the state. We believe that this bond needs to be more clearly recognised by each party, as a compact which makes clear what each contributes and what each gains. Our view of the compact is summarised in Table 1.

Table 1 – Higher education: a new compact

	Contribution	Benefits
Society and taxpayers, as represented by the Government	■ A fair proportion of public spending and national income devoted to higher education. ■ Greater stability in the public funding and framework for higher education.	■ A highly skilled, adaptable workforce. ■ Research findings to underpin a knowledge-based economy. ■ Informed, flexible, effective citizens. ■ A greater share of higher education costs met by individual beneficiaries.
Students and graduates	■ A greater financial contribution than now to the costs of tuition and living costs (especially for those from richer backgrounds). ■ Time and effort applied to learning.	■ More chances to participate in a larger system. ■ Better information and guidance to inform choices. ■ A high quality learning experience. ■ A clear statement of learning outcomes. ■ Rigorously assured awards which have standing across the UK and overseas. ■ Fairer income contingent arrangements for making a financial contribution when in work. ■ Better support for part-time study. ■ Larger Access Funds.
Institutions	■ Collective commitment to rigorous assurance of quality and standards. ■ New approaches to learning and teaching. ■ Continual search for more cost-effective approaches to the delivery of higher education. ■ Commitment to developing and supporting staff.	■ A new source of funding for teaching and the possibility of resumed expansion. ■ New funding streams for research which recognise different purposes. ■ Greater recognition from society of the value of higher education. ■ Greater stability in funding.
Higher education staff	■ Commitment to excellence. ■ Willingness to seek and adopt new ways of doing things.	■ Greater recognition (financial and non-financial) of the value of all of their work, not just research. ■ Proper recognition of their profession. ■ Access to training and development opportunities. ■ Fair pay.
Employers	■ More investment in training of employees. ■ Increased contribution to infrastructure of research. ■ More work experience opportunities for students. ■ Greater support for employees serving on institutions' governing bodies.	■ More highly educated people in the workforce. ■ Clearer understanding of what higher education is offering. ■ More opportunities for collaborative working with higher education. ■ Better accessibility to higher education resources for small and medium size enterprises. ■ Outcomes of research.
The families of students	■ Possible contribution to costs.	■ Better higher education opportunities for their children. ■ Better, more flexible, higher education opportunities for mature students.

The Committee's approach to its work

10. From our first meeting we recognised the scale of the task facing us. We persuaded a number of external members to join working groups to broaden the range of expertise available to us and to help us to advance our work quickly. We gathered as much evidence as possible and heard a wide range of views on the future of higher education. The reports published with our main report describe the outcomes of that work.

11. Throughout our work we received tremendous support and commitment to our task from those within and outside higher education. We cannot name all those who helped us, but we are greatly indebted to every one of them.

Higher education today

12. Higher education in the UK can take justifiable pride in what it has achieved over the last 30 years. It has expanded opportunities: 1.6 million people are students in higher education. Almost a third of young people now go into higher education from school and college, and there are even more mature students than younger ones. Higher education has adapted as the needs of students and other clients have changed. It has maintained its international standing in research, introduced new approaches to learning and teaching and to quality assurance, and has greatly improved its cost-effectiveness. It continues to produce first degree graduates quickly and with low drop-out rates compared to other countries. All this has been achieved through the commitment of those who work in higher education.

13. After a very rapid rise in the number of students between 1988 and 1993, the Government placed a cap on any further growth in publicly-funded full-time undergraduate student numbers, and subsequently withdrew almost all public funding for capital expenditure. Its funding plans for the next three years require further reductions in unit costs. These reductions take place against a background of a unit cost reduction of more than 40 per cent over the last 20 years. This has been achieved, in part, by under-investment in infrastructure. Substantial redundancies are now in prospect and many staff feel that their contribution to the achievements of higher education over the last decade is under-valued. The concern now is that short term pressures to reduce costs, in conditions of no growth, may damage the intrinsic quality of the learning experience which underpins the standing of UK awards.

14. In summary, over the last 20 years:
   - the number of students has much more than doubled;
   - public funding for higher education has increased in real terms by 45 per cent;
   - the unit of funding per student has fallen by 40 per cent;
   - public spending on higher education, as a percentage of gross domestic product, has stayed the same.

15.   Although there is widespread support for the expansion of higher education which has taken place, there are some concerns that current arrangements for quality assurance are not sufficient to ensure comparability of standards in an enlarged sector. Alternative progression routes and qualification aims for a more diverse range of students are not yet fully established. There is also concern that competition between institutions may have hindered beneficial collaboration, and that funding arrangements which reward high quality research have diverted attention from the delivery of high quality teaching.

The wider context

16.   External factors have affected the development of higher education since the Robbins report on higher education in the early 1960s. We judge that external changes will be even more influential over the next 20 years.

17.   Powerful forces – technological and political – are driving the economies of the world towards greater integration. Competition is increasing from developing economies that have a strong commitment to education and training. The new economic order will place an increasing premium on knowledge which, in turn, makes national economies more dependent on higher education's development of people with high level skills, knowledge and understanding, and on its contribution to research. The UK will need to invest more in education and training to meet the international challenge.

18.   However, no public service can automatically expect increasing public expenditure to support it. Higher education needs to demonstrate that it represents a good investment for individuals and society.

19.   The world of work is in continual change: individuals will increasingly need to develop new capabilities and to manage their own development and learning throughout life.

20.   New technology is changing the way information is stored and transmitted. This has implications both for the skills which higher education needs to develop in students, and for the way in which it is delivered. It opens up the possibility of higher education programmes being offered remotely by anyone anywhere in the world, in competition with existing UK institutions, but also offers a global market place in which UK higher education can compete.

21.   As the world becomes ever more complex and fast-changing, the role of higher education as a guardian or transmitter of culture and citizenship needs to be protected. Higher education needs to help individuals and society to understand and adapt to the implications of change, while maintaining the values which make for a civilised society.

22.   Other countries have reached similar conclusions, and other higher education systems are responding. The UK cannot afford to be left behind.

Aims and purposes

23. In the light of these national needs, we believe that the aim of higher education should be to sustain a learning society. The four main purposes which make up this aim are:
    - to inspire and enable individuals to develop their capabilities to the highest potential levels throughout life, so that they grow intellectually, are well equipped for work, can contribute effectively to society and achieve personal fulfilment;
    - to increase knowledge and understanding for their own sake and to foster their application to the benefit of the economy and society;
    - to serve the needs of an adaptable, sustainable, knowledge-based economy at local, regional and national levels;
    - to play a major role in shaping a democratic, civilised, inclusive society.

Future demand for higher education

24. With increasing competition from developed and developing nations, and given the possibility of locating business operations anywhere in the world as a result of the development of communications and information technology, nations will need, through investment in people, to equip themselves to compete at the leading edge of economic activity. In the future, competitive advantage for advanced economies will lie in the quality, effectiveness and relevance of their provision for education and training, and the extent of their shared commitment to learning for life.

25. Demand for higher education from people of all ages will continue to grow. Improvements in educational achievement at school and in further education will increase the number of people ready and willing to move on to higher education. Higher education has proved to be an excellent personal investment with a return averaging between 11 and 14 per cent and we expect it to continue to be a good investment, even after further expansion.

26. While the growing demand for higher education is evident, meeting that demand involves high costs. The national need to expand the present provision must be critically examined. The UK is one of the leaders in the European Union in terms of the proportion of its people graduating. The target set by the last Government for a third of young people to participate in full-time higher education by the year 2000 has already been largely met.

27. As the supply of graduates has expanded rapidly in recent years, the directly measurable national economic return from investment in higher education is expected to fall. Even so, it will still meet the Treasury's required rate of return of six per cent in real terms. We note that participation in higher education by young people in the USA and Japan is much higher than here, although a significant proportion is below first degree level. Some of the nations of the Far East have ambitious plans for expansion. Our visits to France, Germany, the Netherlands, Australia and New Zealand showed a general, long term expectation of expansion. The UK must plan to match the participation rates of other advanced nations: not to do so would weaken the basis of

national competitiveness. Our first conclusion is, therefore, that higher education should resume its growth.

28. We do not see value in any particular target figure for 20 years time. Informed student and employer demand should be the main determinant of the level of participation in the future. But bearing in mind that full-time participation by young people in Scotland and Northern Ireland has risen to around 45 per cent, a rise must be envisaged from the present 32 per cent to a national average of 45 per cent, or more. Within such a total, we believe that much of the expansion should be at sub-degree level, such as study for the Higher National Certificate (HNC) and the Higher National Diploma (HND). At the postgraduate level, especially in the context of lifelong learning, we see a need for continuing expansion in provision for taught higher degrees, at least in line with, and possibly above, the growth in first degree level qualifications.

Recommendation 1   **We recommend to the Government that it should have a long term strategic aim of responding to increased demand for higher education, much of which we expect to be at sub-degree level; and that to this end, the cap on full-time undergraduate places should be lifted over the next two to three years and the cap on full-time sub-degree places should be lifted immediately.**

Widening participation in higher education

29. Despite the welcome increase in overall participation, there remain groups in the population who are under-represented in higher education, notably those from socio-economic groups III to V, people with disabilities and specific ethnic minority groups. Many of the causes lie outside higher education itself, although we recognise that higher education can contribute to improving the situation. We believe that the best progress will be made if the funding of expansion is targeted on institutions which can demonstrate a commitment to widening participation in the recent past, and have a robust strategy for doing so in the future.

Recommendation 2   **We recommend to the Government and the Funding Bodies that, when allocating funds for the expansion of higher education, they give priority to those institutions which can demonstrate a commitment to widening participation, and have in place a participation strategy, a mechanism for monitoring progress, and provision for review by the governing body of achievement.**

30. We also make a number of recommendations designed to allocate funds to institutions and individuals to encourage wider participation.

Students and learning

31. If the future of the UK depends on the quality, effectiveness and relevance of its provision for education and training, it should be a national objective for its teaching and management of learning to be world class. Achievement of this objective does not

require large additional expenditure, and we see no reason why it should not be realised.

32.   But its realisation does depend on a change in the values of higher education, where research is currently the main basis for professional reward and advancement. A survey of academic staff showed that only three per cent of them believed that the payment system rewards teaching, but 63 per cent felt that it should.

33.   There must, therefore, be a radical change in attitudes to teaching.

Recommendation 14   **We recommend that the representative bodies, in consultation with the Funding Bodies, should immediately establish a professional Institute for Learning and Teaching in Higher Education.**

34.   The purpose of this recommendation is to establish higher education teaching as a profession in its own right. The Institute's functions would include accrediting professional achievement in the management of learning and teaching, commissioning research and development work into learning and teaching practices, and stimulating innovation and co-ordinating the development of innovative learning materials. We envisage the Institute taking a leading role in assisting institutions to exploit the potential of communications and information technology for learning and teaching.

35.   Our vision puts students at the centre of the process of learning and teaching. They must have appropriate support and guidance in their academic work, on careers and in other areas if they are to make the most effective use of their investment in higher education. We make a number of detailed recommendations to enhance and support learning.

The nature of programmes

36.   Education after the age of 16 in England, Wales and Northern Ireland is characterised by its close focus on a narrow range of subjects, particularly in the years immediately before entry to higher education. Over the last 30 years, this has been the subject of continuing debate, with proposals to widen the basis of study being frequently advocated. The most recent proposal, in a report by Sir Ron Dearing in 1996, was to offer pupils the option of an Advanced Diploma which combines studies in depth with complementary breadth. We commend this as a way forward.

37.   But our concern in this report is with higher education. The evidence we have had from employers shows that, while the intellectual development that comes from the single honours degree is valued, they see advantage in graduates being able to study their specialism within a broad context. We favour students being able to choose between different types of higher education programme, including more offering a broader knowledge of a range of subjects.

38. There is much evidence of support for the further development of a range of skills during higher education, including what we term the **key** skills of communication, both oral and written, numeracy, the use of communications and information technology and learning how to learn. We see these as necessary outcomes of all higher education programmes.

39. The strongest single message which we received from employers was the value of work experience. This is particularly emphasised by small and medium sized enterprises who need new employees to be able to operate effectively in the workplace from their first day. Further development of work experience opportunities requires action by both employers and institutions.

40. Young people entering higher education will increasingly come with a Progress File which records their achievements up to that point and which is intended for use throughout life. We favour the development of a national format for a transcript of achievement in higher education which students could add to their Progress Files.

41. We have emphasised the need for students and employers to be well-informed about what higher education offers. They need clear statements about the intended outcomes of higher education programmes and the levels at which it is possible to leave with a recognised award.

Recommendation 21   **We recommend that institutions of higher education begin immediately to develop, for each programme they offer, a 'programme specification' which identifies potential stopping-off points and gives the intended outcomes of the programme in terms of:**
- **the knowledge and understanding that a student will be expected to have upon completion;**
- **key skills: communication, numeracy, the use of information technology and learning how to learn;**
- **cognitive skills, such as an understanding of methodologies or ability in critical analysis;**
- **subject specific skills, such as laboratory skills.**

Qualifications and standards

42. Throughout the UK we see the need for a consistent range of awards that recognise achievement. We propose a framework of qualifications which provides for progression, is broad enough to cover the whole range of achievement, is consistent in its terminology, will be well understood within higher education and outside it, and incorporates provision for credit accumulation and, increasingly, scope for the transfer of credits earned in one institution to another.

43. It is fundamental to our approach that awards should be based on achievement, with less emphasis on the length of study required. The framework will cater for a range of aspirations and achievement and enable students to progress through higher levels as

well as to move between programmes. It encompasses vocational and academic qualifications. The framework must have recognised standards at each level, and achieve standing here and abroad. We envisage individuals building up a portfolio of achievements at a range of levels over a working lifetime. The framework of qualifications we propose is set out in Chart 1, with some examples of people moving through the framework in Chart 2.

44. Within the framework, we propose adoption of the Scottish practice, in which the Higher National Certificate and the Higher National Diploma represent achievement at different levels (H1 and H2 in the framework). We see both qualifications as being able to include credit for work-based learning.

45. There is a need to clarify the current confusion over the designation of Masters degrees. We believe that the award of a Masters degree should be reserved for postgraduate research and for taught programmes whose requirements are appropriately more demanding than for a first degree in the subject. We propose the name 'Higher Honours' for advanced undergraduate programmes (such as the present MEng and MPharm).

46. We are particularly concerned to ensure that, when a programme is franchised by one institution to another, the standard required, and the quality of provision offered to the student, is no lower than in the parent institution. As the practice of franchising has expanded rapidly, we are concerned that some further education institutions may have extended themselves too broadly and entered into too many relationships. There have also been a very small number of cases where control by UK higher education institutions of programmes franchised overseas has been inadequate. In the interests of extending opportunity and encouraging lifelong learning, franchising should continue, but only where quality assurance and the maintenance of standards are not prejudiced.

Recommendation 23   We recommend that:
- the Quality Assurance Agency should specify criteria for franchising arrangements;
- these criteria should rule out serial franchising, and include a normal presumption that the franchisee should have only one higher education partner;
- franchising partners should jointly review and, if necessary, amend existing arrangements to ensure that they meet the criteria, and should both certify to the Agency that arrangements conform with the criteria;
- there should be periodic checks by the Agency on the operation of franchise arrangements to verify compliance;
- after 2001, no franchising should take place either in the UK or abroad except where compliance with the criteria has been certified by the Quality Assurance Agency.

Chart 1 – A qualifications framework

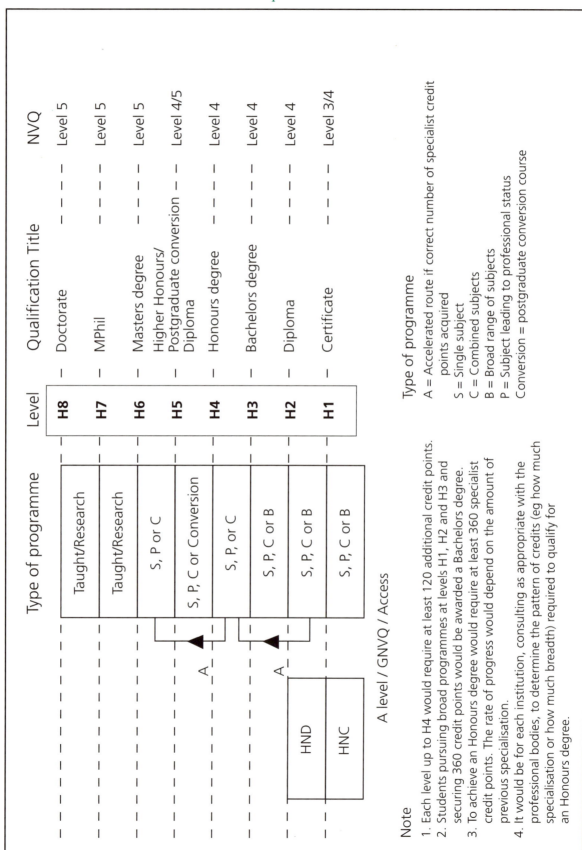

Level	Qualification Title	NVQ	Type of programme
H8	Doctorate	Level 5	Taught/Research
H7	MPhil	Level 5	Taught/Research
H6	Masters degree	Level 5	S, P or C
H5	Higher Honours/ Postgraduate conversion Diploma	Level 4/5	S, P, C or Conversion
H4	Honours degree	Level 4	S, P, or C
H3	Bachelors degree	Level 4	S, P, C or B
H2	Diploma	Level 4	S, P, C or B
H1	Certificate	Level 3/4	S, P, C or B

A level / GNVQ / Access

HND

HNC

Type of programme
A = Accelerated route if correct number of specialist credit points acquired
S = Single subject
C = Combined subjects
B = Broad range of subjects
P = Subject leading to professional status
Conversion = postgraduate conversion course

Note
1. Each level up to H4 would require at least 120 additional credit points.
2. Students pursuing broad programmes at levels H1, H2 and H3 and securing 360 credit points would be awarded a Bachelors degree.
3. To achieve an Honours degree would require at least 360 specialist credit points. The rate of progress would depend on the amount of previous specialisation.
4. It would be for each institution, consulting as appropriate with the professional bodies, to determine the pattern of credits (eg how much specialisation or how much breadth) required to qualify for an Honours degree.

Chart 2 – Examples of routes through the framework

Student A had always been interested in English and wanted to study it in depth in higher education. Having acquired the relevant A levels, she entered higher education as a full-time student and followed the single subject route and left with an honours degree at level H4. She takes no breaks and completes her Honours degree in three years by the accelerated route.

Student B was interested in science, but less sure about the specific area she wanted to study. She entered higher education and studied a General Sciences programme up to level H2 on a full-time basis. She left full-time studies with a diploma having got a job as a technician in a laboratory. She continued her studies on a part-time basis sponsored by her employer focusing on biology and acquired an Honours degree at level H4.

Student C, following a Short Service Commission in the Army, wanted to retrain as a primary school teacher, specialising in education of young children. He enrolled on a BEd programme, which enabled him to study for a profession and acquire a range of subject knowledge. He left with an Honours degree at level H4. Later, in order to progress in his career and update his skills, he enrolled on a part-time MEd programme. This took him up to level H6.

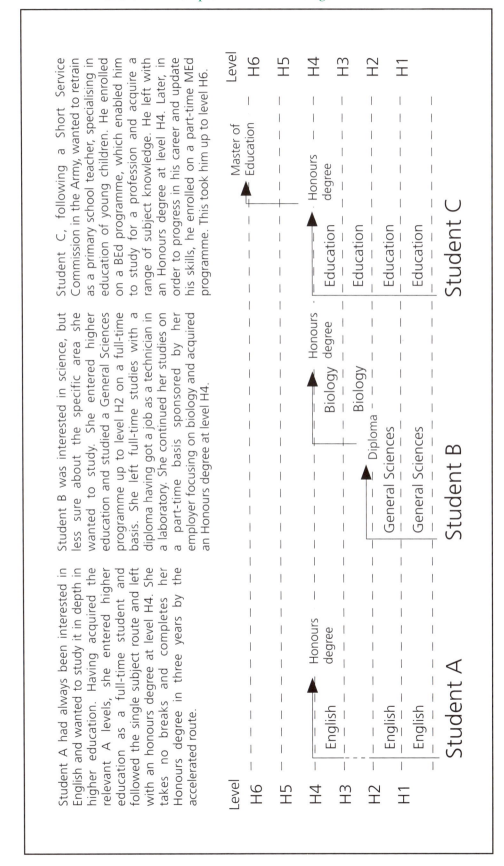

Level	Student A	Student B	Student C
H6			Master of Education
H5			
H4	Honours degree — English	Honours degree — Biology	Honours degree — Education
H3	English	Biology	Education
H2	English	Diploma — General Sciences	Education
H1	English	General Sciences	Education

47. Expansion in student numbers must not be at the cost of lowering the standards required for awards. Nor should it result in lowering the quality of provision or in increasing numbers of drop-outs or failures. Higher education in the UK has a long-established reputation for quality and standards. It is because of this reputation that the UK currently attracts so many students from overseas. We owe it to them, and to our own students, that the quality of their learning should be high and that the awards they gain carry respect. The three year honours degree is short by world standards, and its international acceptability depends on the quality of the learning experience and high standards for awards.

48. We welcome the establishment of the Quality Assurance Agency to oversee quality and standards in higher education, but believe that it should have a somewhat different agenda from that currently proposed.

Recommendation 24   **We recommend that the representative bodies and Funding Bodies amend the remit of the Quality Assurance Agency to include:**
- **quality assurance and public information;**
- **standards verification;**
- **the maintenance of the qualifications framework;**
- **a requirement that the arrangements for these are encompassed in a code of practice which every institution should be required formally to adopt, by 2001/02, as a condition of public funding.**

49. The external examiner system, through which institutions seek to ensure common standards for their awards, worked well in a small community of institutions. It is inadequate to meet the needs of the much expanded and more diverse system of higher education that we now have. We need to build from established practice to create a more effective mechanism through which, while awards remain the responsibility of the individual institution, there is acceptance that the general standard of awards is a shared responsibility of the whole academic community.

Recommendation 25   **We recommend to the Quality Assurance Agency that its early work should include:**
- **to work with institutions to establish small, expert teams to provide benchmark information on standards, in particular threshold standards, operating within the framework of qualifications, and completing the task by 2000;**
- **to work with universities and other degree-awarding institutions to create, within three years, a UK-wide pool of academic staff recognised by the Quality Assurance Agency from which institutions must select external examiners;**
- **to develop a fair and robust system for complaints relating to educational provision;**
- **to review the arrangements in place for granting degree-awarding powers.**

50. To the extent that higher education adopts these recommendations, the need for the apparatus of quality assessment and audit by the Quality Assurance Agency will be correspondingly reduced.

51. We welcome participation by professional bodies in establishing the standards appropriate to their discipline. We particularly urge them to be actively engaged in accrediting programmes and in working with the academic community to specify required outcomes. We share the concerns of some professions about the required entry standards for programmes. However assessments at the end of the first or second year should form the basis on which decisions on progress to a degree should be based. We refer in our main report to particular concerns about entry standards for degree programmes in engineering.

Supporting scholarship and research

52. We have identified four distinct purposes for research in higher education. These are:
    - to add to the sum of human knowledge and understanding;
    - to inform and enhance teaching;
    - to generate useful knowledge and inventions in support of wealth creation and an improved quality of life;
    - to create an environment in which researchers can be encouraged, and given a high level of training.

53. It has been notable that over the last decade there has been no increase in real terms in Government funding for research. Research expenditure in the UK compares unfavourably with that in many competitor countries. Yet the evidence available to us shows the UK is among the world leaders in both the quality and the quantity of research outputs and is cost-effective in the use of resources. The importance of the research base to the national economy, and its cost-effectiveness, provides a strong case for increasing the present level of funding.

54. We have devised a series of principles for research funding allocation to support the purposes. The mechanisms for distributing funding should be clear and transparent. Excellence should be supported, and where research is funded, it should be funded adequately.

55. There is an urgent need to put right past under-investment in the research infrastructure. The resources must be found to enable the UK to maintain its place as one of the world's major research centres. Without it, our universities will no longer be able to attract funding from industry or international institutions on the scale they have in the past. Nor will they continue to be valued partners with overseas institutions in research.

56. We also consider it necessary that funding policies to support research should promote, as far as possible, high quality teaching. We endorse the policy of targeting funding on high quality departments, but there is also a need for funding to support the research and scholarship which underpin teaching in those departments which do not aspire to be at the leading edge in research.

57. Funding should also support applied and regional research work. We think that it is in the national interest to bring industry and higher education into stronger partnership in both research and its exploitation, for their mutual benefit. This should be encouraged by the Government.

Recommendation 34 **We recommend:**
- **to the Government that, with immediate effect, projects and programmes funded by the Research Councils meet their full indirect costs and the costs of premises and central computing, preferably through the provision of additional resources;**
- **to the Funding Bodies that the next Research Assessment Exercise is amended to encourage institutions to make strategic decisions about whether to enter departments for the Exercise or whether to seek a lower level of non-competitive funding to support research and scholarship which underpins teaching;**
- **to the Government that an Industrial Partnership Development Fund is established immediately to attract matching funds from industry, and to contribute to regional and economic development;**
- **to the Government that it promotes and enables, as soon as possible, the establishment of a revolving loan fund of £400 to £500 million, financed jointly by public and private research sponsors, to support infrastructure in a limited number of top quality research departments which can demonstrate a real need.**

58. To obtain the best use of resources, human and physical, stronger arrangements are required to promote joint and collaborative activities by institutions and interdisciplinary work.

59. There is a need for better support for research in the arts and humanities and propose the establishment of an Arts and Humanities Research Council

60. For research students, there is need for a code of practice to guide institutions and inform students on what they can reasonably expect. We endorse the proposals made to that end in the 'Review of postgraduate education' chaired by Professor Martin Harris.

The local and regional role of higher education

61. Higher education is now a significant force in regional economies, as a source of income and employment, in contributing to cultural life, and in supporting regional and local economic development. This is brought out strongly in the report of our Scottish Committee: it is no less recognised in Wales and Northern Ireland. In England, regional consciousness varies, but we recognise the significance of the contribution of higher education to the localities and wider areas in which they are situated.

62. The contribution of individual institutions to regions and localities is diverse. It includes support through research and consultancy, attracting investment and

providing new sources of employment, meeting labour market needs, supporting lifelong learning, and contributing to the quality of life as centres of culture.

63. As part of the compact we envisage between higher education and society, each institution should be clear about its mission in relation to local communities and regions. We note that the Government is likely to create regional chambers which will develop an economic strategy for regions and establish regional development agencies.

Recommendation 36   **We recommend to the Government that institutions of higher education should be represented on the regional bodies which it establishes, and that the Further Education Funding Council regional committees should include a member from higher education.**

64. We make proposals that higher education institutions should be able to bid for regional sources of funds, to enable them to be responsive to the needs of local industry and commerce, and should seek ways of giving firms, especially small and medium sized enterprises, easy and co-ordinated access to information about higher education services in their areas. We also make recommendations designed to help foster entrepreneurship among students and staff in higher education.

Communications and Information technology

65. Throughout our report we identify scope for the innovative use of new Communications and Information Technologies (C&IT) to improve the quality and flexibility of higher education and its management. We believe these give scope for a reduction in costs. In the short term, implementation requires investment in terms of time, thought and resources, and we make recommendations about how this might be achieved.

66. The full exploitation of C&IT by higher education institutions will require senior management to take an imaginative leap in devising a strategy for their institutions which can bring about this change. The Funding Bodies and the Government can help to encourage such a development.

Recommendation 41   **We recommend that all higher education institutions in the UK should have in place overarching communications and information strategies by 1999/2000.**

67. The UK already enjoys a good information technology infrastructure, and we make recommendations about how this might be completed and maintained. The main challenge for the future is to harness that infrastructure, together with high quality materials and good management, to meet the needs of students and others.

68. The use of new technologies for learning and teaching is still at a developmental stage but we expect that students will soon need their own portable computers as a means of access to information and for learning via a network. We are also aware that students will need access to high quality networked desktop computers that permit the use of the latest multi-media teaching materials and other applications.

Recommendation 46   We recommend that by 2000/01 higher education institutions should ensure that all students have open access to a Networked Desktop Computer, and expect that by 2005/06 all students will be required to have access to their own portable computer.

Staff in higher education

69.   The health of higher education depends entirely on its staff, whether academic, professional or administrative. There is concern among staff that they have received neither the recognition, opportunities for personal development, nor the rewards which their contribution over the last decade merits. Over the next 20 years, the roles of staff are likely to change, as they undertake different combinations of functions at different stages of their careers. To support and prepare staff for these new working patterns, more focused and appropriate training and staff development activities will be needed.

Recommendation 47   We recommend that, over the next year, all institutions should:
- review and update their staff development policies to ensure they address the changing roles of staff;
- publish their policies and make them readily available for all staff;
- consider whether to seek the Investors in People award.

70.   To achieve world class higher education teaching, it should become the norm for all permanent staff with teaching responsibilities to be trained on accredited programmes.

Recommendation 48   We recommend to institutions that, over the medium term, it should become the normal requirement that all new full-time academic staff with teaching responsibilities are required to achieve at least associate membership of the Institute for Learning and Teaching in Higher Education, for the successful completion of probation.

71.   In this era of continuing change the rewards offered must be sufficient to recruit, retain and motivate staff of the required quality. Recent evidence suggests that the majority, but by no means all, of staff in higher education are paid substantially below comparable private and public sector rates. On the other hand, there is evidence of an increase in the ratio of senior lecturer to lecturer posts, which may have offset a relative decline in academic salary levels. There is, however, growing concern about the present arrangements for determining pay and conditions of service. Central pay bargaining is under strain, as many institutions feel the need to take decisions in relation to their own circumstances rather than collectively. Others argue for maintaining national bargaining, a statutory pay review body or a standing review body.

72.   Whatever view may be taken of the various options, the issue of remuneration should not be looked at in isolation. Significant changes will be needed as higher education responds to changing needs and opportunities. To the extent that higher levels of remuneration may be justified, there is the question of how institutions can meet the

cost. The employment framework of all higher education staff, not just academics, needs to be addressed. These are material issues and we think the time has come for a review of the whole framework within which pay, conditions of service, work practices and the use of human resources can be settled. Our main report suggests terms of reference for such a review.

Recommendation 50   **We recommend to the higher education employers that they appoint, after consultation with staff representatives, an independent review committee to report by April 1998 on the framework for determining pay and conditions of service. The Chairman should be appointed on the nomination of the Government.**

Management and governance of higher education institutions

73.   The effectiveness of any organisation depends upon the effectiveness of its management and governance arrangements. We have identified three principles to underpin management and governance in higher education institutions. These are that:
- institutional autonomy should be respected;
- academic freedom within the law should be protected;
- governance arrangements should be open and responsive.

74.   Although institutions have made impressive improvements in efficiency in the face of a dramatic fall in public funding per student over the last 20 years, the challenge to find new and better ways of doing things will continue and intensify. Some institutions currently fall far short of the performance of the best. Our main report considers how institutions might make better use of their staff, their estates, their equipment and other resources.

75.   Over the next 20 years, communications and information technology will provide increasing opportunities to improve institutional effectiveness and efficiency. A continuing challenge to management will be to realise the full potential of such systems.

76.   We are conscious of the enormous contribution that members of governing bodies make to institutions. They serve higher education well. But we are also aware that there is great diversity in governance arrangements, and sometimes a lack of clarity. Although we do not seek uniformity, we believe that institutions may often be able to achieve greater clarity and effectiveness in the way they govern themselves. We make recommendations to this effect. In particular, we propose a code of practice on governance, and, as part of that, we think that, as a general rule in the interests of effectiveness, membership of a governing body should not exceed 25. To gain maximum benefit from the work of governing bodies, we see a need for them to review their own performance, along with that of their institution.

Recommendation 57 We recommend that each governing body should systematically review, at least once every five years, with appropriate external assistance and benchmarks:

- its own effectiveness and, where there is in excess of 25 members, show good reason why a larger body is needed for its effectiveness;
- the arrangements for discharging its obligations to the institution's external constituencies;
- all major aspects of the institution's performance, including the participation strategy.

The outcomes of the review should be published in an institution's annual report. The Funding Bodies should make such a review a condition of public funding.

The pattern of institutions which provide higher education

77.   The names and distribution of institutions are important matters that go to the heart of the capacity of the system to deliver higher education. For the future pattern of institutions to have public confidence, it should be guided by a number of principles: the need for diversity; institutional autonomy; responsiveness to national need; allowance for the development of individual institutions; the need for access across the country; and the need for proper economy and quality of provision.

78.   We support the existing diversity between institutions, believing it to be a considerable strength in responding to the diverse needs of students as participation in higher education widens. We recommend that funding arrangements should reflect and support such diversity. Notwithstanding this, diversity must not be an excuse for lower standards or poor quality provision for students. We believe there should be greater control on the use of institutional titles, so that students, employers and others are clear about the status of institutions. We make recommendation on this issue and on the use of the title 'university'.

79.   We considered the special role of further education colleges in providing sub-degree higher education, and believe that growth and transfer of this provision to these colleges should be encouraged.

Recommendation 67 We recommend to the Government and the Funding Bodies that, in the medium term, priority in growth in sub-degree provision should be accorded to further education colleges; and that, wherever possible:

- more sub-degree provision should take place in further education colleges;
- higher education provision in further education colleges should be funded directly;
- there should be no growth in degree level qualifications offered by further education colleges.

80.   We have considered the case for establishment of additional universities, and concluded that there should be a systematic decision-making process for deciding whether individual cases are reasonable.

81.   Many of those giving evidence advanced the case for greater collaboration between institutions to improve effectiveness and efficiency throughout the sector. We found no obvious external factors that were discouraging institutions from collaborating, and found many examples of such practice. However, given the importance of collaboration, it will be important that there are no unnecessary barriers to it.

Recommendation 68   **We recommend to the Funding Bodies and the Research Councils that they review their mainstream teaching and research funding arrangements to ensure they do not discourage collaboration between institutions; and that, where appropriate, they encourage collaboration. We recommend to the Funding Bodies that they be prepared to use their funds on a revolving basis, bringing forward and offsetting annual allocations in support of collaboration which has a strong educational and financial rationale.**

The funding requirement

82.   We have looked critically at both the short and long term funding requirements of the higher education sector.

83.   The present public spending plans for higher education assume a reduction in real terms of expenditure per student of 6.5 per cent over the two years 1998-99 and 1999-2000. This is in addition to the more than 40 per cent reduction achieved since 1976. Furthermore, the Government decided, from 1995-96, to reduce substantially capital funding for equipment and the refurbishment of institutions' estates. We have considered how far this is sustainable without significant damage to the quality of the student experience and to the research base. We have concluded that institutions should be able to manage a one per cent a year real reduction in funding per student over the next two years; a 6.5 per cent reduction would damage quality.

84.   Overall, we have identified a range of short term funding needs for the sector:
   - an alleviation of the proposed cut in funding per student;
   - infrastructure requirements;
   - changes to existing student support levels;
   - the resumed growth in student numbers we have recommended.

85.   In total, we estimate that an additional £350 million in 1998-1999 and £565 million in 1999-2000 is required.

86.   For the long term, we have identified six elements requiring additional expenditure if the higher education system is to develop effectively over the next 20 years. These are:
   - an expansion of student numbers to allow around 45 per cent of young people to participate full-time and corresponding increases in the numbers of mature students, postgraduates and those who study part-time;
   - providing part-time students with better support and thereby encouraging growth in lifelong learning;
   - adequate infrastructure;

- proper funding to support all the purposes of research and for an Arts and Humanities Research Council;
- improving maintenance support for students, including larger Access Funds;
- increasing higher education pay in line with earnings elsewhere in the economy.

87. We think it right that levels of student support should be kept under review to avoid exacerbating the financial problems which some students already face.

Recommendation 70 **We recommend to the Government that it reviews annually the total level of support for student living costs taking into account the movement of both prices and earnings.**

88. The additional quantified funding requirements measured in 1995-96 prices are summarised in Table 2.

Table 2: Summary of additional annual funding requirement in 20 years time compared to current expenditure

	£ million (recurrent) 1995-96 prices
1. Increased student numbers offset by savings	800
2. Equity for part-time undergraduate students	50
3. Refurbishing the estate and replacing and improving equipment (including C&IT equipment)	250
4. Research	185
5. Access Funds and improvements to support for disabled students	40
6. Real growth salaries	600
Total	1,925

89. The net addition of close to £2 billion takes into account an offsetting saving of £1,300 million. This is a demanding requirement. The long and short term funding requirements have to be regarded as a minimum, because they do not allow for any significant increases in the volume of publicly funded research despite the need for the UK economy to be knowledge-based or for research to underpin higher level teaching. Nor do they include quantified sums for any real increase in pay resulting from the immediate pay review we recommend or the cost of increasing student support by more than the Retail Prices Index.

Who should pay for higher education?

90. There is widespread recognition of the need for new sources of funding for higher education. The costs of higher education should be shared among those who benefit from it. We have concluded that those with higher education qualifications are the main beneficiaries, through improved employment prospects and pay. As a consequence, we suggest that graduates in work should make a greater contribution to

the costs of higher education in future. Employer contributions to higher education and training should mainly take the form of a contribution to the cost of continuing education and training for their employees.

91. The state should also remain a major source of funding for higher education in the future because:
- it has a direct interest in ensuring that participation in the UK matches that of its competitors;
- it needs to ensure that tomorrow's workforce is equipped with the widest range of skills and attributes;
- it must ensure that access to opportunities for individuals to benefit from higher education is socially just;
- it needs to secure the economic and cultural benefits which higher education can offer the whole nation.

92. We have noted the Government's desire, over the long term, to increase the proportion of national wealth devoted to education and training and believe that higher education should share in this.

Recommendation 71 We recommend to the Government that, over the long term, public spending on higher education should increase with the growth in Gross Domestic Product.

Funding learning and teaching

93. Public funding for tuition currently flows to institutions via block grants from the Funding Bodies and tuition fees for full-time undergraduate students which are paid through those students' mandatory awards. Over the long term a greater proportion of public funding should follow informed student choice so that institutions have greater rewards for responding to that demand.

Recommendation 72 We recommend to the Government that it shifts the balance of funding, in a planned way, away from block grant towards a system in which funding follows the student, assessing the impact of each successive shift on institutional behaviour and the control of public expenditure, with a target of distributing at least 60 per cent of total public funding to institutions according to student choice by 2003.

94. Institutions told us that the suddenness with which funding changes were introduced were sometimes almost as difficult to manage as the required reductions in public funding. We believe that greater stability would enable institutions to plan more effectively.

Recommendation 73 We recommend to the Government that the public funding for higher education institutions should be determined on a rolling three year basis.

Student support and graduate contributions

95. A student support system for the future should, as far as possible:
    - be equitable, and encourage broadly based participation;
    - require those with the means to do so to make a fair contribution to the costs of their higher education;
    - support lifelong learning, so that choices between part-time and full-time study and for discontinuous study are financially neutral;
    - be easy to understand, administratively efficient and cost-effective.

96. Although levelling up of support for those groups of students, particularly part-time students, who are currently less well-supported is desirable, it would be very expensive and might risk substituting public support for the support currently provided by employers and others well-placed to do so. Reducing support for those who are currently better supported could involve hardship for individuals, especially if changes were introduced rapidly without time for them to prepare. We have taken a pragmatic approach to devising arrangements which support students and enable graduates in work to make a contribution.

97. Part-time undergraduates currently have to make a contribution to their tuition costs and they are not generally eligible for public support for their living costs. Although many are supported by their employers, there are disincentives to study for the unemployed and for those on low incomes.

Recommendation 76 — We recommend to the Government that:
- **from 1998/99 it should enable institutions to waive tuition fees for part-time students in receipt of Jobseeker's Allowance or certain family benefits;**
- **as part of its forthcoming review of the social security system, it should review the interaction between entitlement to benefits and part-time study, with a view to ensuring that there are no financial disincentives to part-time study by the unemployed or those on low incomes;**
- **it should extend eligibility for Access Fund payments to part-time students from 1998/99, and additional funding should be made available for this purpose.**

98. Although the average graduate receives a good financial return from higher education, some will experience periods of unemployment, some will need to take career breaks, and others will have low paid jobs. If graduates are to be asked to make an increased contribution they need the reassurance that they will not be faced with unreasonable payment burdens. This can be achieved by introducing payment mechanisms which relate the annual level of payment to a graduate's income: income contingent payments.

Recommendation 78 — We recommend to the Government that it introduces, by 1998/99, income contingent terms for the payment of any contribution towards living costs or tuition costs sought from graduates in work.

99. There are a number of ways of operating an income contingent contribution scheme, including:

- a graduate tax under which graduates are liable to pay an income tax supplement;
- a deferred contribution scheme;
- a loan scheme under which individuals could choose to pay the required contribution upfront or take out a loan which would be repayable after graduation.

100. A graduate tax is attractive because it has the potential to secure large additional resources for higher education, but it provides no means by which individuals can pay their contribution upfront, and thus does not deliver additional funding in the short term. For the graduate, it is open-ended, resulting in those who are particularly successful being expected to contribute large sums. For institutions, it would not guarantee that the income from the tax would benefit them because, to do so, would cut across the general principle that tax revenue is not earmarked for particular services.

101. A deferred contribution scheme would involve a student making a commitment, on enrolment, subsequently to contribute a certain percentage of his or her income with the total potential contribution being limited to the cost of the higher education programme taken or some defined percentage of that. The terms of the payments would be set, however, so that the average graduate would, in practice, pay only around 25 per cent of the cost. Only those who secured the highest incomes would pay back the full cost of their higher education programmes. Like a graduate tax this has the potential to deliver substantial extra resources, but the graduate contribution is not open-ended. Like the graduate tax it would not release resources in the short term. This disadvantage might be overcome by offering the option of paying at the time of study or of making a contribution later. These options are worth further exploration for the medium term, but we do not think that they could be introduced quickly.

102. We examined a range of options for supporting graduates to make contributions by providing loans during study to be repaid on an income contingent basis by the graduate once in work.

103. The widespread view in evidence was that an additional contribution from graduates should be sought by converting the existing support for student living costs from 50:50 grants and loans to 100 per cent loans. We looked carefully at this option. But we also examined three others which involve graduates making a contribution to their tuition costs because we felt that such contributions offer a number of advantages over the more widely canvassed alternative. We return to these advantages in paragraph 108. The four options are summarised in Table 3.

Table 3: Graduate contribution options

	Living costs support	Tuition contribution
Existing system	50% means tested grant 50% loan	None
Option A: Maintenance contribution	100% income contingent loan	None
Option B: Tuition contribution	50% means tested grant 50% income contingent loan	25% contribution with income contingent loan
Option C: Means tested tuition contribution	100% income contingent loan	25% means tested contribution with no loan
Option D: Tuition contribution with restoration of maintenance grants	100% means tested grant	25% contribution with income contingent loan

104. We reviewed each option against the impact it would have on: individuals and their families at the time of study; graduates; different social groups; and the funds generated for higher education.

105. Table 4 summarises the range of parental contribution required for a student who studies away from home outside London for three years. For simplicity, rounded figures of £10,000 for the maximum support for living costs over three years and £1,000 a year for a tuition contribution, where appropriate, are used. The table shows clearly that the distinctive feature of Option A is that it removes any obligation from higher income families to contribute to the costs of higher education for their children.

Table 4: Assumed parental/family contributions for three years under different options

	Existing system	Maintenance contribution	Tuition contribution	Means tested tuition contribution	Tuition contribution with restoration of maintenance grant
		A	B	C	D
Higher income families (£)	5,000	0	5,000	3,000	10,000
Middle income families (£)	2,000	0	2,000	1,200	4,000
Lower income families (£)	0	0	0	0	0

106. Table 5 shows, on the same basis, the maximum graduate commitment which would be incurred by a student who studied for three years. We do not believe any of these commitments would be unmanageable for graduates so long as income contingent payment mechanisms were in place.

Table 5: Graduate commitment for three years study (£)

Existing system	Maintenance contribution	Tuitionl contribution	Means tested tuition contribution	Tuition contribution with restoration of maintenance grants
	A	B	C	D
5,000	10,000	8,000	10,000	3,000

107. Table 6 shows how the various options redistribute public subsidies among families of different incomes.

Table 6: Effect of options on distribution of public subsidies for three years study compared to present polices

	Students from high income families	Students from low income families
A: Maintenance contribution	Increased public subsidy through availability of additional £5,000 living cost loans at a subsidised rate.	Decreased public subsidy as living costs grants of £5,000 replaced by loans at a subsidised rate.
B: Tuition contribution	Decreased public subsidy, through £3,000 tuition contribution, backed by a subsidised loan.	Decreased public subsidy, through £3,000 tuition contribution, backed by a subsidised loan.
C: Means tested tuition contribution	Depends precisely on the balance between the increased public subsidy on living cost loans and the level of the new tuition contribution.	Decreased public subsidy as living cost grants of £5,000 replaced by loans at a subsidised rate.
D: Tuition contribution with restoration of maintenance grant	Decreased public subsidy through loss of £5,000 subsidised loans for maintenance and new tuition contribution of £3,000, although the latter is mitigated by access to a subsidised loan.	Depends on the precise balance between increased public subsidy in 100 per cent grant for living costs and loss of public subsidy in having to contribute £3,000 to tuition backed by a subsidised loan. Likely to be an increase in public subsidy.

108. We would be particularly reluctant to see any reduction in public subsidies being concentrated on students from the poorest families and even more reluctant to see the funding released by this, and more, being used to increase the subsidies for others.

109. Table 7 shows what net contribution each of the options makes to public finances on both the present cash accounting basis for public finances and the planned resource accounting basis. Negative numbers represent an additional outflow of public funds.

Table 7: Financial effects of options compared to existing arrangements.

A. Cash accounting					
£million Net contribution to public finances by academic year in 1995-96 prices					
	Year 1	Year 2	Year 3	Year 8	Year 18
A: Maintenance contribution	(200)	(300)	(400)	(50)	800
B: Tuition contribution	50	100	150	500	1,100
C: Means tested tuition contribution	0	0	50	400	1,450
D: Tuition contribution with restoration of maintenance grant	200	300	450	650	600
B. Resource accounting					
£million Net contribution to public finances by academic year in 1995-96 prices					
A: Maintenance contribution	350	500	700	450	100
B: Tuition contribution	350	550	750	700	900
C: Means tested tuition contribution	550	850	1,100	950	750
D: Tuition contribution with restoration of maintenance grant	100	150	150	300	800

Notes: Figures in brackets are net additional costs to the Exchequer.

Cash accounting counts all loans advanced as public expenditure in the year they are made and all repayments as negative public expenditure in the year they are received. Resource accounting counts as public expenditure only the implied subsidies in the loans (including interest subsidies, provision for default and other kinds of non-payment).

110. The main conclusion from this table is that none of the options provides the additional resources needed in the long term by higher education. Option A is particularly limited in this respect. We have concluded that any option which delivered the resources needed would produce unacceptable burdens on graduates and on families of modest means, or would lead to unacceptably high levels of graduate debt.

111. There are arguments for all four options but we have concluded that, on balance, Option B offers the best balance between seeking a continuing contribution from higher income families and from graduates in work. As the figures show, seeking an increased contribution from graduates towards living costs as in Option A:
   - takes away subsidies from the poorest families and redirects them to others;
   - increase public expenditure in the short term;
   - releases modest resources for higher education in the long term.

   We strongly favour options which involve a contribution to tuition costs for three further reasons:
   - students are likely to be more demanding of institutions if they are contributing;
   - it would help to level the playing field between full- and part-time study and would put full-time higher education students on a more similar basis to adult further education students;
   - if graduates are contributing to the costs of their tuition there will be a clearer expectation that the funding released should be spent on higher education.

112. We suggest that the contribution should be a flat rate one and not varied by subject of study so that access to expensive or prestigious programmes is by academic merit not financial means. The contribution should, by analogy with the contribution expected from adult further education students, be of the order of 25 per cent of average tuition costs each year. Government bursary or scholarship arrangements may be needed for subjects such as medicine and teacher education where courses are longer than three years but generally the contribution required should be proportional to the number of years of study. In order to protect against precipitate increases in the level of expected contribution, there should be a thorough review before any such change could be made by the Government.

Recommendation 79 **On a balance of considerations, we recommend to the Government that it introduces arrangements for graduates in work to make a flat rate contribution of around 25 per cent of the average cost of higher education tuition, through an income contingent mechanism, and that it ensures that the proportion of tuition costs to be met by the contribution cannot be increased without an independent review and an affirmative resolution of both Houses of Parliament. The contributions made by graduates in work in this way should be reserved for meeting the needs of higher education.**

113. We suggest that the Government considers either offering a discount for upfront payment or introducing a modest real rate of interest on loans to encourage those who can afford it to make a contribution at the time of study

114. Because none of the options we explored delivers the additional resources needed in the short term and the Government has indicated that additional public funding will not be forthcoming, we looked at the possibility of seeking greater contributions from the only other immediately available source, students' parents. Our main report discusses two variants, of Options B and C, which have an increased means test. Both would release substantial extra sums. The decision on their social acceptability is essentially a political one.

115. A fundamental problem with the Government providing loans for students is their treatment in the national accounts. Under conventional Government Accounting a loan is treated exactly like a grant in the year in which it is made. The planned introduction of a new form of accounting, resource accounting, will make clearer the fact that grants and loans are not equivalent. There will still, however, be a problem in that loans will continue to count against the Public Sector Borrowing Requirement in the year that are advanced. This is not the approach adopted in all other countries.

Recommendation 80 **We recommend to the Government that it looks urgently at alternative and internationally accepted approaches to national accounting which do not treat the repayable part of loans in the same way as grants to students.**

116. The previous Government explored various ways to secure private finance for student loans. We are not satisfied that any such approach offers value for money.

Enabling individuals to make their contributions

117.　Any future mechanism to support individuals in making their contribution should be easy to understand, simple to administer, efficient and cost-effective. As the Inland Revenue already has in place arrangements for assessing income and securing payments from almost all the working population we believe that it would be best-placed to collect income contingent payments on behalf of our proposed Student Support Agency (see below).

Recommendation 82　**We recommend to the Government that the Inland Revenue should be used as the principal route for the collection of income contingent contributions from graduates in work, on behalf of the Student Loans Company.**

118.　Currently there are a number of different organisations involved in student support, including 160 local education authorities, a central awards organisation in Scotland, Education and Library Boards in Northern Ireland, and the Student Loans Company. This is not clear or simple for students or for institutions. We believe that the there should be a single Student Support Agency which might be built up from the existing Student Loans Company.

Recommendation 83　**We recommend to the Government that it establishes, as soon as possible, a unified Student Support Agency with responsibility for:**
- **assessing the eligibility of individuals for various kinds of public support;**
- **administering graduate contributions on an income contingent basis;**
- **means testing and paying grants for students' living costs;**
- **making per capita tuition payments to institutions according to the number of students they enrol.**

119.　Such a unified Student Support Agency would cover many of the functions which are sometimes suggested for a system of individual learning accounts (ILAs) or a Learning Bank. However much more work is required to define the exact nature of such accounts. They could provide a mechanism for giving incentives to individuals and their families to save for higher education (although the case for going beyond current financial instruments is not a strong one); and to give incentives to employers to contribute to their employees' development through higher level study. We expect that, over time, individuals, with the development of lifelong learning, will expand their use of existing tax efficient savings mechanisms for education. ILAs as part of a wider strategy on education and training should provide added incentives for employers to contribute within the context of the expansion of continuing professional development.

Government and higher education institutions

120.　We see great value in maintaining the long-standing practice of the Government remaining at arms' length from individual institutions and therefore in retaining intermediary Funding Bodies. This practice should be extended to Northern Ireland.

But we also see advantage in progressively channelling an increasing proportion of funding for tuition through students and, thereby, encouraging institutions to be more responsive to student requirements.

121. This will require students to be able to make an informed choice based on information about the offerings of higher education, its likely costs, and possible future employment opportunities. Students need better information and we recommend that their representatives with the representative bodies of schools, colleges and higher education institutions should together identify what information is needed and how it can be provided, making appropriate use of information technology.

122. To develop a coherent approach to the development of the whole of post-18 education we recommend that the funding arrangements in Wales, in which funding councils for higher and further education are served by a common executive, are adopted in Scotland and Northern Ireland. In England the scale of activity is such that we see a continuing need for two separate funding councils with their own executives, but we welcome the moves already in hand to secure some greater co-ordination of action at a regional level

123. Higher education is now a such major element in the national economy that a UK-wide review is needed on a regular basis.

Recommendation 88 **We recommend to the Government that, in five years' time and subsequently every ten years, it constitutes a UK-wide independent advisory committee with the task of assessing the state of higher education, advising the Government on its financing, and on ways in which, in future years, it can best respond to national needs; on any action that may be needed to safeguard the character and autonomy of institutions; and in particular any changes required in the level of student support and contributions from graduates in employment.**

Higher education in Scotland, Wales and Northern Ireland

124. Although our terms of reference relate to the whole of the UK, we are conscious of the distinctive needs and traditions of higher education in the different parts of the country. Higher education in Northern Ireland and Wales is broadly similar to that in England. However, higher education provision in Scotland has a number of particularly distinct features. For this reason we established a Scottish Committee to advise us – its report is published with our main report.

125. One particular feature that we have noted about higher education in Scotland is the breadth of undergraduate degree programmes in comparison with the rest of the UK. Scotland has a high participation rate of nearly 45 per cent, with much of the difference between it and the rest of the UK attributable to sub-degree level work. We use the experience of Scotland in relation to both of these issues to inform our report more widely.

126. Higher education in Wales is similar to that in England, although a distinctive feature is the large amount of residential full-time provision because of the dependence of institutions on students coming to study from outside the vicinity of the institution. Having worked to enhance the quality of its research provision, we heard that Wales intends to increase the volume of research in order to attract inward investment and to support economic regeneration.

127. There are only two universities and two colleges of higher education in Northern Ireland. A serious issue for the Province is that 40 per cent of young people have to leave to take up higher education opportunities. A considerable number of these do not do so from choice, but because of the limitation on the number of places and the relatively high standard of entry to the local universities. This issue has prompted us to include an appendix addressing particular issues facing Northern Ireland, and proposing a number of options for increasing the provision of places in a cost effective way.

Next steps

128. Our report sets out a major programme of change for higher education over the next twenty years. Our vision for the future is clear. Although our outlook has been to the long term, our detailed recommendations necessarily focus on the first steps towards that vision. We hope that the legacy of our work will be a higher education system which is well-placed to develop and respond as new challenges and circumstances arise, including those which we cannot foresee from the perspective of 1997. Our recommendations add up to a coherent package for the future of higher education. We do not intend that those to whom they are addressed should choose to implement only some of them. The new compact requires commitment from all sides.

129. We have addressed our recommendations to those who should, in our view, be responsible for taking them forward. Where it is possible to set a specific timescale for the necessary action, we have done so. Some of our recommendations require organisations to undertake substantial developmental work before they can be implemented, and some are of less immediate urgency than others. We are conscious of the need not to overload organisations with too many tasks at once: it is often better to focus energy and attention on the most important and urgent work, but that does not mean that our recommendations for the medium and longer term can be ignored. Recommendations which we have described as for implementation 'over the medium term' are those which should generally be implemented within the next three to five years, although work in preparation for that may well need to start immediately. Those recommendations which we suggest should be implemented 'over the long term' are those which require even more substantial preparatory work or the prior implementation of other recommendations before they can be put into effect. Most of them are unlikely to be implemented in less than five years.

130. The recommendations are addressed to a wide range of bodies who have varying responsibilities in relation to higher education. Table 8 shows the allocation.

Table 8: Organisations to whom recommendations are addressed.

Organisation	Recommendation number
The Government	1, 2, 5, 6, 7, 11, 19, 22, 29, 34, 35, 36, 37, 39, 43, 44, 51, 54, 55, 56, 61, 62, 63, 64, 65, 66, 67, 70, 71, 72, 73, 74, 76, 77, 78, 79, 80, 81, 82, 83, 84, 85, 86, 87, 88, 90, 91, 92, 93
Higher Education Funding Bodies	2, 3, 4, 6, 7, 14, 24, 26, 27, 28, 32, 33, 34, 44, 57, 58, 59, 61, 66, 67, 68, 75
Further Education Funding Bodies	3, 7
The Institute for Learning and Teaching in Higher Education	6, 13, 15
The Higher Education Statistics Agency	7
Institutions and their governing bodies	8, 9, 11, 12, 13, 16, 17, 18, 20, 21, 31, 38, 39, 40, 41, 42, 45, 46, 47, 48, 49, 50, 51, 52, 57, 60
Representative bodies of Higher Education	10, 14, 22, 24, 26, 38, 51, 53, 54, 58
The Quality Assurance Agency	11, 22, 23, 25, 69
Students' unions	12
Employer representative bodies	19, 38
Awarding bodies and the organisations which oversee them	22
Franchising partners	23
Companies	30
Research Councils	32, 68

131. We give below some guidance on the immediate priorities for action.

Funding

132. There is an immediate short term problem with the funding of higher education. If this is not addressed by the Government, there is a real danger that some institutions will be severely damaged and that others will take unilateral action, for example through the introduction of supplementary fees, which will make it impossible for our long-term vision to be realised.

133. If the Government accepts our proposals on funding, it will need to introduce primary legislation because it does not currently have the power to make loans to support of students' tuition costs or to give effect to our proposals for income-contingent collection of loan repayments. This must be a priority if additional resources are to flow to higher education in 1998-99. We are encouraged that the Government has already indicated its intention of introducing early legislation.

134. The same degree of urgency will need to be applied to the complex process of implementation. If implementation on this timescale cannot be achieved, alternative means of providing additional resources in the short term will have to be found, but the options are not attractive. We have already said that short-term moves to remove student loans from the public sector are unlikely to represent good value for money. The only other immediate source of resources, apart from the taxpayer, is parents of students.

135. Our proposals on funding do not stand in isolation. They are part of a new compact between all the stakeholders of higher education. The Government must therefore commit itself just as firmly and with the same urgency to the other elements of that compact, if all who are involved in higher education are to be encouraged play their part. This means that the early legislation we propose must provide for a procedure to govern any review of the contribution to be made by graduates. The Government must also ensure that new arrangements are well-publicised and explained clearly to prospective students and their families.

136. Universities and colleges have pressed hard for a solution to the funding crisis which they perceive. We have made proposals which should place them on a firmer financial footing. But institutions need to take urgent action too. They owe it to students and to the taxpayer to make sure that they make the best possible use of the available resources. They must secure appropriate management and cost information systems to support this as quickly as possible. They will need the help of the Funding Bodies and their representative bodies to ensure that all know what the best can do. Work on developing appropriate benchmarks is urgent. Institutions must ensure that their governance arrangements enable them to carry forward the development we propose.

Quality and standards

137. In return for additional contributions from graduates, institutions must make much clearer what they offering to students. They must work continually to improve the quality of teaching and they must approach the mutual assurance of standards with real commitment. Anything less would be to sell their students short. The immediate requirement from institutions is that, acting collectively, they give the Quality Assurance Agency all the support and facilities it needs to be fully effective and that they establish the Institute for Learning and Teaching in Higher Education, and give it the necessary support and facilities too.

138. Our recommendations place great expectations on the new Quality Assurance Agency. The bodies which established the Agency need urgently to review and amend its remit if it is to assume the role we propose for it. It needs the support of the whole sector in its tasks and it will need to embark very rapidly on a large programme of work. New systems for the assurance of quality and standards must be in place and seen to be effective within a short space of time. If they are not, the Government will be justified in intervening to protect the interests of students.

Research

139. The priorities in research are to begin to rectify the deficiencies of the infrastructure and to establish new arrangements which encourage strategic decisions by institutions to concentrate on their strengths. The Government will need to take immediate steps to secure private sector contributions for the rolling loan fund for infrastructure: we have already identified some organisations who are willing in principle to contribute. The Funding Bodies need to set the rules for the next Research Assessment Exercise quickly so that institutions can begin now to plan their preparation for it.

Staff in higher education

140. Staff in higher education have achieved much in recent years and our report expects that they will continue to be dedicated, professional and adaptable. They must be given appropriate support in this. Our recommendations for more systematic staff development and training, and especially for accreditation of teaching staff need to be pursued as a matter of urgency by individual institutions and by the sector collectively. The overall review of pay and conditions of service which we recommend should also be set up as soon as possible, in order to try to avoid a repetition of the unsatisfactory pay negotiations seen this year.

Higher education's local and regional role

141. We assume that the Government will be taking early steps to introduce new regional structures. As it does so, it needs to take account of our recommendation that higher education should be represented on the new bodies and it must ensure that higher education can play its full part in economic regeneration.

Conclusion

142. We know, from all the contacts we have had in our work, that the value and importance of higher education is widely recognised. We also know that those within higher education are committed to its wellbeing and are willing to embrace change. If all that good will, energy and professionalism can be focused on the developments proposed in this report, we are convinced that UK higher education will match the best in the world over the next 20 years.

List of Recommendations

Chapters 1–5
NONE

Chapter 6

1 We recommend to the Government that it should have a long term strategic aim of responding to increased demand for higher education, much of which we expect to be at sub-degree level; and that to this end, the cap on full-time undergraduate places should be lifted over the next two to three years and the cap on full-time sub-degree places should be lifted immediately.

Chapter 7

2 We recommend to the Government and the Funding Bodies that, when allocating funds for the expansion of higher education, they give priority to those institutions which can demonstrate a commitment to widening participation, and have in place a participation strategy, a mechanism for monitoring progress, and provision for review by the governing body of achievement.

3 We recommend that, with immediate effect, the bodies responsible for funding further and higher education in each part of the UK collaborate and fund – possibly jointly – projects designed to address low expectations and achievement and to promote progression to higher education.

4 We recommend that the Funding Bodies consider financing, over the next two to three years, pilot projects which allocate additional funds to institutions which enrol students from particularly disadvantaged localities.

5 We recommend to the Government that:
   - it considers the possibility of restoring to full-time students some entitlement to social security benefits, as part of its forthcoming review of the social security system. This review should include consideration of two particular groups in current difficulty, those who temporarily withdraw from higher education due to illness and those with dependent children aged over 16;
   - the total available to institutions for Access Funds should be doubled with effect from 1998/99 and that the scope of the funds should be extended to facilitate participation by students who would otherwise be unable to enter higher education.

6 We recommend:
   - to the Funding Bodies that they provide funding for institutions to provide learning support for students with disabilities;
   - to the Institute for Learning and Teaching in Higher Education (see Recommendation 14) that it includes the learning needs of students with disabilities in its research, programme accreditation and advisory activities;

■ to the Government that it extends the scope of the Disabled Students Allowance so that it is available without a parental means test and to part-time students, postgraduate students and those who have become disabled who wish to obtain a second higher education qualification.

7   We recommend that further work is done over the medium term, by the further and higher education Funding Bodies, the Higher Education Statistics Agency, and relevant government departments to address the creation of a framework for data about lifelong learning, using a unique student record number.

Chapter 8

8   We recommend that, with immediate effect, all institutions of higher education give high priority to developing and implementing learning and teaching strategies which focus on the promotion of students' learning.

9   We recommend that all institutions should, over the medium term, review the changing role of staff as a result of Communications and Information Technology, and ensure that staff and students receive appropriate training and support to enable them to realise its full potential.

10   We recommend that, over the medium term, the representative bodies, in consultation with other relevant agencies, should seek to establish a post-qualification admissions system.

11   We recommend that:
     ■ institutions of higher education, over the medium term, integrate their careers services more fully into academic affairs and that the provision of careers education and guidance is reviewed periodically by the Quality Assurance Agency;
     ■ the Government, in the medium to long term, should integrate careers advice for lifelong learning, to complement services based inside higher education institutions.

12   We recommend to students' unions and institutions that they review, on a regular basis, the services offered to their students and adapt them as necessary, in particular to meet the needs of part-time students.

13   We recommend that institutions of higher education begin immediately to develop or seek access to programmes for teacher training of their staff, if they do not have them, and that all institutions seek national accreditation of such programmes from the Institute for Learning and Teaching in Higher Education.

14   We recommend that the representative bodies, in consultation with the Funding Bodies, should immediately establish a professional Institute for Learning and Teaching in Higher Education. The functions of the Institute would be to accredit programmes of training for higher education teachers; to commission research and development in learning and teaching practices; and to stimulate innovation.

15   We recommend that the Institute should:
- develop, over the medium term, a system of kitemarking to identify good computer-based learning materials;
- co-ordinate the national development, over the medium and long term, of computer-based learning materials, and manage initiatives to develop such materials;
- facilitate discussion between all relevant interest groups on promoting the development of computer-based materials to provide common units or modules, particularly for the early undergraduate years.

Chapter 9

16   We recommend that all institutions of higher education should, over the medium term, review the programmes they offer:
- with a view to securing a better balance between breadth and depth across programmes than currently exists;
- so that all undergraduate programmes include sufficient breadth to enable specialists to understand their specialism within its context.

17   We recommend to institutions of higher education that, over the medium term, their admission procedures should develop to value good levels of competence in communication, numeracy and the practical use of information technology.

18   We recommend that all institutions should, over the medium term, identify opportunities to increase the extent to which programmes help students to become familiar with work, and help them to reflect on such experience.

19   We recommend that the Government, with immediate effect, works with representative employer and professional organisations to encourage employers to offer more work experience opportunities for students.

20   We recommend that institutions of higher education, over the medium term, develop a Progress File. The File should consist of two elements:
- a transcript recording student achievement which should follow a common format devised by institutions collectively through their representative bodies;
- a means by which students can monitor, build and reflect upon their personal development.

21   We recommend that institutions of higher education begin immediately to develop, for each programme they offer, a 'programme specification' which identifies potential stopping-off points and gives the intended outcomes of the programme in terms of:
- the knowledge and understanding that a student will be expected to have upon completion;
- key skills: communication, numeracy, the use of information technology and learning how to learn;
- cognitive skills, such as an understanding of methodologies or ability in critical analysis;
- subject specific skills, such as laboratory skills.

Chapter 10

22   We recommend that the Government, the representative bodies, the Quality Assurance Agency, other awarding bodies and the organisations which oversee them, should endorse immediately the framework for higher education qualifications that we have proposed.

23   We recommend that:
- the Quality Assurance Agency should specify criteria for franchising arrangements;
- these criteria should rule out serial franchising, and include a normal presumption that the franchisee should have only one higher education partner;
- franchising partners should jointly review and, if necessary, amend existing arrangements to ensure that they meet the criteria, and should both certify to the Agency that arrangements conform with the criteria;
- there should be periodic checks by the Agency on the operation of franchise arrangements to verify compliance;
- after 2001, no franchising should take place either in the UK or abroad except where compliance with the criteria has been certified by the Quality Assurance Agency.

24   We recommend that the representative bodies and Funding Bodies amend the remit of the Quality Assurance Agency to include:
- quality assurance and public information;
- standards verification;
- the maintenance of the qualifications framework;
- a requirement that the arrangements for these are encompassed in a code of practice which every institution should be required formally to adopt, by 2001/02, as a condition of public funding.

25   We recommend to the Quality Assurance Agency that its early work should include:
- to work with institutions to establish small, expert teams to provide benchmark information on standards, in particular threshold standards, operating within the framework of qualifications, and completing the task by 2000;
- to work with universities and other degree-awarding institutions to create, within three years, a UK-wide pool of academic staff recognised by the Quality Assurance Agency, from which institutions must select external examiners;
- to develop a fair and robust system for complaints relating to educational provision;
- to review the arrangements in place for granting degree-awarding powers.

26   We recommend to the representative bodies and the Funding Bodies that the Board of the Quality Assurance Agency should, as soon as possible, include a student and an international member.

Chapter 11

27   We recommend that the Funding Bodies, through the Joint Information Systems Committee (JISC), should continue to manage and fund, on a permanent basis, quality and cost-effective Communications and Information Technology (C&IT) services for researchers and should, in due course, introduce charges for services on a volume-of-usage basis.

28 We recommend to the Funding Bodies that the Joint Information Systems Committee (JISC) should be invited to report, within a year, on options to provide sufficient protected international bandwidth to support UK research.

29 We recommend to the Government that a new Arts and Humanities Research Council (AHRC) should be established as soon as possible.

30 We recommend that companies should take a strategic view of their relationship with higher education and apply the same level of planning to it that they give to other aspects of their operations.

31 We recommend to institutions of higher education that they should, over the next two years, review their postgraduate research training to ensure that they include, in addition to understanding of a range of research methods and training in appropriate technical skills, the development of professional skills, such as communication, self-management and planning.

32 We recommend that the Funding Bodies and the Research Councils commission a study to evaluate the funding of interdisciplinary research, including the incentives and disincentives. The report should be ready to inform the next Research Assessment Exercise.

33 We recommend to the Funding Bodies that, in the interests of transparency and applying international standards properly, the practice of including one or more international members in all Research Assessment Exercise (RAE) panels, wherever possible, should be introduced to the next RAE.

34 We recommend:
- to the Government that, with immediate effect, projects and programmes funded by the Research Councils meet their full indirect costs and the costs of premises and central computing, preferably through the provision of additional resources;
- to the Funding Bodies that the next Research Assessment Exercise is amended to encourage institutions to make strategic decisions about whether to enter departments for the Exercise or whether to seek a lower level of non-competitive funding to support research and scholarship which underpins teaching;
- to the Government that an Industrial Partnership Development Fund is established immediately to attract matching funds from industry, and to contribute to regional and economic development;
- to the Government that it promotes and enables, as soon as possible, the establishment of a revolving loan fund of £400 to £500 million, financed jointly by public and private research sponsors, to support infrastructure in a limited number of top quality research departments which can demonstrate a real need.

35 We recommend to the Government that it should establish, as soon as possible, a high level independent body to advise the Government on the direction of national policies for the public funding of research in higher education, on the distribution and level of such funding, and on the performance of the public bodies responsible for distributing it.

Chapter 12

36   We recommend to the Government that institutions of higher education should be represented on the regional bodies which it establishes, and that the Further Education Funding Council regional committees should include a member from higher education.

37   We recommend to the Government that funding should continue to be available after April 1998, when the present provision from the Higher Education Regional Development Fund is due to cease, to support human capital projects which enable higher education to be responsive to the needs of local industry and commerce.

38   We recommend to higher education institutions and their representative bodies that they examine, with representatives of industry, ways of giving firms, especially small and medium sized enterprises, easy and co-ordinated access to information about higher education services in their area.

39   We recommend:
- to the Government that it considers establishing a modest fund to provide equity funding to institutions to support members of staff or students in taking forward business ideas developed in the institution, and to support the creation of incubator units;
- to higher education institutions that they establish more technology incubator units within or close to the institution, within which start-up companies can be fostered for a limited period until they are able to stand alone.

40   We recommend to higher education institutions that they consider the scope for encouraging entrepreneurship through innovative approaches to programme design and through specialist postgraduate programmes.

Chapter 13

41   We recommend that all higher education institutions in the UK should have in place overarching communications and information strategies by 1999/2000.

42   We recommend that all higher education institutions should develop managers who combine a deep understanding of Communications and Information Technology with senior management experience.

43   We recommend to the Government that it should review existing copyright legislation and consider how it might be amended to facilitate greater ease of use of copyright materials in digital form by teachers and researchers.

44   We recommend to the Government and the Funding Bodies that, to harness and maximise the benefits of Communications and Information Technology, they should secure appropriate network connectivity to all sites of higher education delivery and further education colleges by 1999/2000, and to other relevant bodies over the medium term.

45   We recommend that institutions of higher education, collectively or individually as appropriate, should negotiate reduced tariffs from telecommunications providers on behalf of students as soon as possible.

46   We recommend that by 2000/01 higher education institutions should ensure that all students have open access to a Networked Desktop Computer, and expect that by 2005/06 all students will be required to have access to their own portable computer.

Chapter 14

47   We recommend that, over the next year, all institutions should:
- review and update their staff development policies to ensure they address the changing roles of staff;
- publish their policies and make them readily available for all staff;
- consider whether to seek the Investors in People award.

48   We recommend to institutions that, over the medium term, it should become the normal requirement that all new full-time academic staff with teaching responsibilities are required to achieve at least associate membership of the Institute for Learning and Teaching in Higher Education, for the successful completion of probation.

49   We recommend that all institutions should, as part of their human resources policy, maintain equal opportunities policies, and, over the medium term, should identify and remove barriers which inhibit recruitment and progression for particular groups and monitor and publish their progress towards greater equality of opportunity for all groups.

50   We recommend to the higher education employers that they appoint, after consultation with staff representatives, an independent review committee to report by April 1998 on the framework for determining pay and conditions of service. The Chairman should be appointed on the nomination of the Government.

51   We recommend to the Government, institutions, and the representative bodies of higher education, that, over the long term, the superannuation arrangements for academic staff should be harmonised by directing all new entrants to the Universities Superannuation Scheme.

Chapter 15

52   We recommend to institutions that, over the medium term, they develop and implement arrangements which allow staff and external bodies to have access to and understand the true costs of research.

53   We recommend that the Committee of Vice-Chancellors and Principals, in collaboration with other institutional representative bodies, reviews the functions of the Universities and Colleges Information Systems Association to ensure that it can promote the implementation of Communications and Information Technology in management information systems.

54   We recommend that the Government, together with representative bodies, should, within three years, establish whether the identity of the governing body in each institution is clear and undisputed. Where it is not, the Government should take action to clarify the position, ensuring that the Council is the ultimate decision-making body, and that the Court has a wider representative role, to inform decision-making but not to take decisions.

55   We recommend to the Government that it takes action so that:
      - individuals may not serve as members of a governing body for more than two terms, unless they also hold office;
      - it is a requirement for the governing body at each institution to include student and staff membership and a majority of lay members;
      - an individual may not chair a governing body for more than two terms of office.

56   We recommend that the Government takes the lead, with the Privy Council, in discussions with institutional representatives to introduce, within three years, revised procedures capable of responding more quickly to an institution requesting a change in the size of its governing body. The intention should be to ensure a response within one year.

57   We recommend that each governing body should systematically review, at least once every five years, with appropriate external assistance and benchmarks:
      - its own effectiveness and, where there is in excess of 25 members, show good reason why a larger body is needed for its effectiveness;
      - the arrangements for discharging its obligations to the institution's external constituencies;
      - all major aspects of the institution's performance, including the participation strategy.
      The outcomes of the review should be published in an institution's annual report. The Funding Bodies should make such a review a condition of public funding.

58   We recommend that, over the medium term, to assist governing bodies in carrying out their systematic reviews Funding Bodies and representative bodies develop appropriate performance indicators and benchmarks for families of institutions with similar characteristics and aspirations.

59   We recommend to the Funding Bodies that they require institutions, as a condition of public funding, to publish annual reports which describe the outcomes of the governing body's review and report on other aspects of compliance with the code of practice on governance.

60   We recommend to institutions that, over the next two years, they review and, if necessary, amend their arrangements for handling complaints from students, to ensure that: they reflect the principles of natural justice; they are transparent and timely; they include procedures for reconciliation and arbitration; they include an independent, external element; and they are managed by a senior member of staff.

Chapter 16

61   We recommend to the Government and the Funding Bodies that diversity of institutional mission, consistent with high quality delivery and the responsible exercise of institutional autonomy, should continue to be an important element of the United Kingdom's higher education system; and that this should be reflected in the funding arrangements for institutions.

62   We recommend to the Government that it takes action as soon as possible to end the scope for a confusion between the title and the name used by institutions, either through clarifying the legal position or by ensuring that conditions can be placed on the flow of public funds so that these go only to those institutions which agree to restrict their use of a name and title to that to which they are legally entitled.

63   We recommend to the Government that, in the medium term, there is no change to the current criteria for university status; but that, for the future, there should be a period of relative stability in the number of universities with the weight accorded to the numerical criteria reduced and greater emphasis placed on a distinctive role and characteristics in awarding this status; and that the Government should give notice of this.

64   We recommend to the Government that it takes action, either by amending the powers of the Privy Council or by ensuring that conditions can be placed on the flow of public funds, to enable the removal of degree-awarding powers where the Quality Assurance Agency demonstrates that the power to award degrees has been seriously abused.

65   We recommend to the Government that it takes action, either by clarifying the legal position or by ensuring that conditions can be placed on the flow of public funds, to restrict the use of the title 'University College' to those institutions which are in every sense a college which is part of a university under the control of the university's governing body; and to those higher education institutions which have been granted taught degree awarding powers.

66   We recommend to the Government and the Funding Bodies that there is greater clarity about where responsibility lies for decisions about the establishment of new universities; and that criteria are developed for deciding such cases and allocating public funding.

67   We recommend to the Government and the Funding Bodies that, in the medium term, priority in growth in sub-degree provision should be accorded to further education colleges; and that, wherever possible:
■ more sub-degree provision should take place in further education colleges;
■ higher education provision in further education colleges should be funded directly;
■ there should be no growth in degree level qualifications offered by further education colleges.

68   We recommend to the Funding Bodies and the Research Councils that they review their mainstream teaching and research funding arrangements to ensure they do not discourage collaboration between institutions; and that, where appropriate, they encourage collaboration. We recommend to the Funding Bodies that they be prepared to use their funds on a revolving basis, bringing forward and offsetting annual allocations in support of collaboration which has a strong educational and financial rationale.

69   We recommend to the Quality Assurance Agency that, as it develops its arrangements, it ensures that these arrangements do not discourage collaboration between institutions.

Chapter 17
70   We recommend to the Government that it reviews annually the total level of support for student living costs taking into account the movement of both prices and earnings.

Chapter 18
71   We recommend to the Government that, over the long term, public spending on higher education should increase with the growth in Gross Domestic Product.

Chapter 19
72   We recommend to the Government that it shifts the balance of funding, in a planned way, away from block grant towards a system in which funding follows the student, assessing the impact of each successive shift on institutional behaviour and the control of public expenditure, with a target of distributing at least 60 per cent of total public funding to institutions according to student choice by 2003.

73   We recommend to the Government that the public funding for higher education institutions should be determined on a rolling three year basis.

74   We recommend to the Government that variations in the level of public funding for teaching, outside modest margins, should occur only where:
- there is an approved difference in the provision;
- society, through the Secretary of State or his or her agent, concludes, after examining an exceptionally high level of funding, that in relation to other funding needs in higher education, it represents a good use of resources.

75   We recommend to the Funding Bodies that they should explore the possibility of setting aside some of their total grant, as soon as possible, to establish revolving loan schemes to fund:
- projects to refurbish buildings (to improve fitness for purpose) or to undertake large scale long term maintenance projects;
- expensive equipment purchases (for teaching or research);
- collaborative projects which will facilitate access for staff and students in a region to teaching or research facilities which could not otherwise be provided on a viable basis.

Chapter 20

76 We recommend to the Government that:

- from 1998/99 it should enable institutions to waive tuition fees for part-time students in receipt of Jobseeker's Allowance or certain family benefits;
- as part of its forthcoming review of the social security system, it should review the interaction between entitlement to benefits and part-time study, with a view to ensuring that there are no financial disincentives to part-time study by the unemployed or those on low incomes;
- it should extend eligibility for Access Fund payments to part-time students from 1998/99, and additional funding should be made available for this purpose.

77 We recommend to the Government that, once the interim bursary scheme expires, it establishes permanent arrangements for the equitable support of students of dance, drama and stage management at institutions which are not in receipt of public funds.

78 We recommend to the Government that it introduces, by 1998/99, income contingent terms for the payment of any contribution towards living costs or tuition costs sought from graduates in work.

79 On a balance of considerations, we recommend to the Government that it introduces arrangements for graduates in work to make a flat rate contribution of around 25 per cent of the average cost of higher education tuition, through an income contingent mechanism, and that it ensures that the proportion of tuition costs to be met by the contribution cannot be increased without an independent review and an affirmative resolution of both Houses of Parliament. The contributions made by graduates in work in this way should be reserved for meeting the needs of higher education.

80 We recommend to the Government that it looks urgently at alternative and internationally accepted approaches to national accounting which do not treat the repayable part of loans in the same way as grants to students.

81 We recommend to the Government that Scottish students who have had only one year's education after statutory schooling, many of whom under current arrangements would choose to take a four year honours degree, should not make a tuition contribution for one of their years in higher education. Beyond that, this would be a matter for consideration by the Secretary of State for Scotland.

Chapter 21

82 We recommend to the Government that the Inland Revenue should be used as the principal route for the collection of income contingent contributions from graduates in work, on behalf of the Student Loans Company.

83 We recommend to the Government that it establishes, as soon as possible, a unified Student Support Agency with responsibility for:

- assessing the eligibility of individuals for various kinds of public support;
- administering graduate contributions on an income contingent basis;
- means testing and paying grants for students' living costs;

■ making per capita tuition payments to institutions according to the number of students they enrol.

Chapter 22

84   We recommend to the Government that the tradition of institutional separation from national and sub-national levels of government is firmly maintained; and that this principle is extended to Northern Ireland.

85   We recommend to the Government that, with immediate effect, it brings together the representative bodies of students, schools, colleges, higher education institutions and the organisations offering careers services to identify what better information is needed by students about higher education opportunities, their costs and benefits; and to work together to improve timely dissemination of the information.

86   We recommend to the Government that the division of responsibility between the further and higher education Funding Bodies in England and Wales should be such that the higher education Funding Bodies are responsible for funding all provision defined as higher education.

87   We recommend to the Government that the Teacher Training Agency continue its remit in respect of teacher training in England but that the respective responsibilities of the Higher Education Funding Council for England and the Teacher Training Agency are reviewed in drawing up proposals for the role of a General Teaching Council.

88   We recommend to the Government that, in five years' time and subsequently every ten years, it constitutes a UK-wide independent advisory committee with the task of assessing the state of higher education; advising the Government on its financing and on ways in which, in future years, it can best respond to national needs; on any action that may be needed to safeguard the character and autonomy of institutions; and, in particular, on any changes required in the level of student support and contributions from graduates in employment.

Chapter 23
NONE

Chapter 24
NONE

Appendix 1

89   We recommend that higher education institutions in Northern Ireland, in close collaboration with all the relevant external players, steadily enhance their regional role, taking full advantage of the special potential for the development of strong regional networks.

90   We recommend to the Government that options be examined for substantially increasing the number of higher education places in Northern Ireland in a cost-effective way which involves no compromise in quality and standards.

91   We recommend to the Government and institutions that consideration be given to adopting the Dearing 16–19 year olds option as one of the bases for entrance to universities in Northern Ireland.

92   We recommend to the Government that the scale and nature of funding for research in Northern Ireland universities should be assessed afresh in the context of the Province's strategy for economic development and of the recommendations in Chapter 11

93   We recommend to the Government that there be constituted in Northern Ireland a Tertiary Education Forum, a Higher Education Funding Council and a Further Education Funding Council.